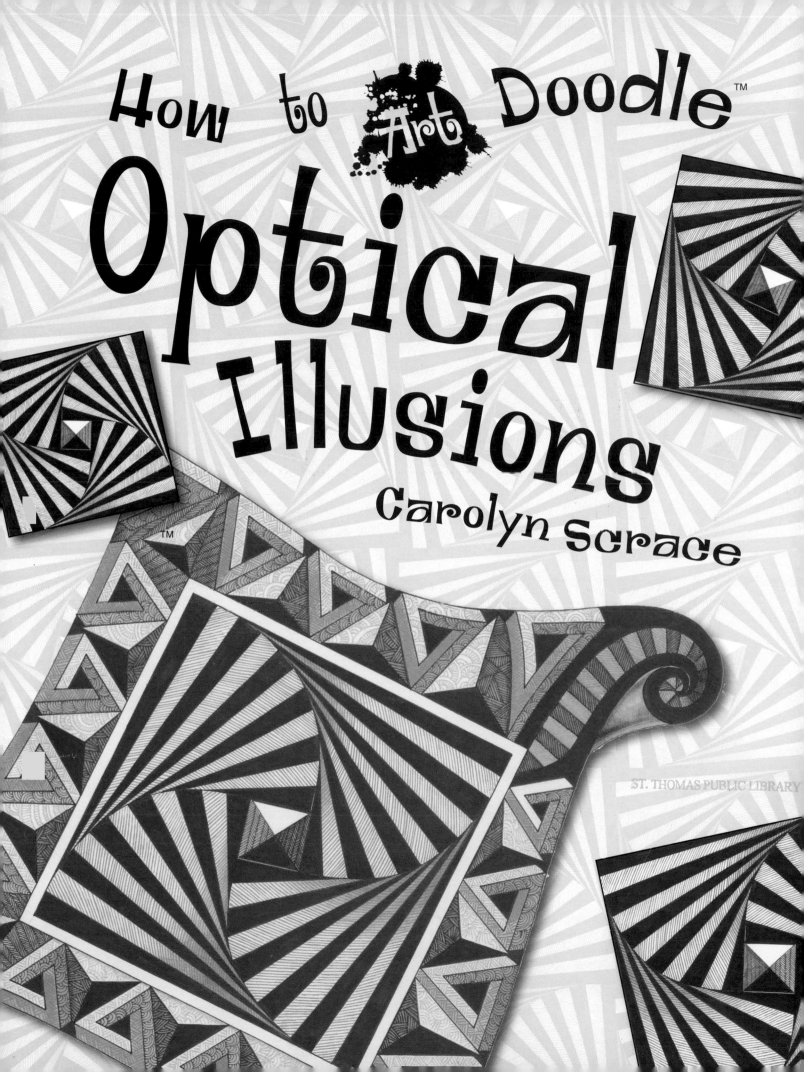

How to Art Doodle™
Optical Illusions

Carolyn Scrace

This edition first published in MMXV by
Book House

Distributed by Black Rabbit Books
P.O. Box 3263
Mankato
Minnesota MN 56002

© MMXV The Salariya Book Company Ltd
Printed in the United States of America.
Printed on paper from sustainable forests.

Cataloging-in-Publication Data is available
from the Library of Congress

HB ISBN: 978-1-909645-48-6
PB ISBN: 978-1-910184-35-6

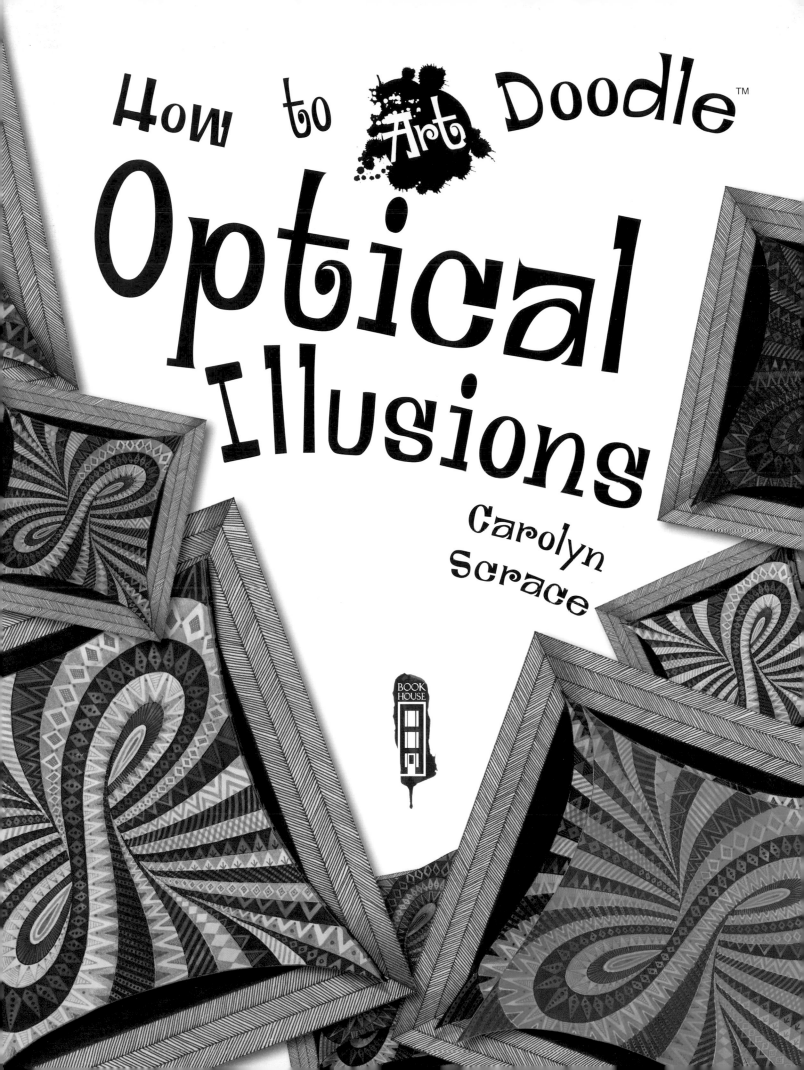

How to Art Doodle™

Optical Illusions

Carolyn Scrace

BOOK HOUSE

Contents

Please note: Sharp blades and scissors should be used under adult supervision.

Introduction

Art Doodling releases creativity and develops drawing skills. Discover the thrill of using simple Art Doodle patterns to build up a stunning optical illusion. These pages are packed with inspirational ideas and designs that show how easily amazing 3D effects can be achieved.

Do it anywhere

Art Doodling can be done anywhere, and needs no special equipment. Some of the best Art Doodles are often drawn on the backs of receipts or paper napkins!

The unexpected

Optical illusions can be found in the world around you. Often we see what we expect to see. Have fun seeing everyday things in a different and unexpected way!

Inspiration

Take a look at the work of M. C. Escher, an artist famous for his optical illusions. Another inspiring artist renowned for painting illusions is Salvador Dalí, whose surreal work is inspirational. Street art can also be a terrific source of ideas for optical illusions.

Art Doodling
optical illusions

Optical illusions are images that appear different from reality. In other words, our perception of what our eyes and brain are seeing differs from what actually exists. Images that seem to be one thing are, in fact, something entirely different. Illusions happen when our eyes are tricked into seeing an image wrongly.

Impossible objects

This triangular shape just cannot exist, yet our brain accepts it as real. The brain processes the three cube shapes and the three bar shapes, then wrongly interprets the two-dimensional shapes as a three-dimensional object.

Optical trickery

Four simple curved lines and converging stripes create this incredible optical illusion (left). The design works best when simple Art Doodles are used to decorate it. Turn to pages 18–19 for a step-by-step guide to drawing this optical trickery!

Crazy colors

Vivid, contrasting colors add tremendous impact to an optical illusion. This design consists of a broken figure eight. It creates an irresistible illusion of depth in a flat, two-dimensional design. The curved stripes provide fantastic shapes for Art Doodling. Turn to pages 16–17 for a step-by-step guide to drawing this optical illusion.

Pencil sharpener

Eraser

Graphite pencils come in different grades, from hard to soft. The softer the pencil, the darker the mark it makes.

Thick **marker pens** are perfect for filling in large areas. Fine **permanent marke**r pens are great for outlines and details.

Tools & materials

There are no special tools and materials needed for Art Doodling. An old pencil stub and a scrap of paper are all you need to get started! You may, however, wish to use some or all of the tools and materials suggested here. It's important to experiment and try to use whatever tools and materials inspire you.

Pencil crayons are ideal for adding soft shading to an area. Use them for coloring in.

Felt-tip pens come in a range of thicknesses. Thick pens are ideal for blocking-in large areas of color.

Fineliner pens produce a flowing line. They come in a wide range of colors and are ideal for intricate doodling.

A black gel pen is useful for outlines and detailed doodles. **Metallic and white gel pens** are ideal for doodling onto colored paper or over dark-colored Art Doodles.

8

Compasses are used for drawing circles and arcs. (Alternatively, cups and saucers make an ideal substitute.)

Sketchpad for jotting down ideas and trying out designs.

Use your sketchbook for experimenting with new techniques, and keep notes of what materials you used.

Types of paper

Cartridge paper comes in a variety of weights. Heavyweight paper is good for water-based paint. Note: Ink lines may bleed on some cartridge papers.

Bristol board or **paper** may be textured or smooth. Smooth Bristol board is good to work on with pencils, pencil crayons, markers, felt-tips, and gcl and fineliner pens for adding fine details.

Palette (or clean saucer) for mixing paint.

Paintbrushes come in a wide range of sizes.

Watercolor paints and **colored inks** are ideal for covering large areas of a design with subtle color.

Gouache is opaque watercolor. Use it for painting plain, flat borders.

Light & shade

Adding areas of shading to Art Doodled shapes can make them appear solid. Scribbled, hatched, and crosshatched lines are just some of the techniques that can be used to add tone.

Technique

Scribbling is great for shading various textures. To create dark tones, simply make the scribbles denser.

Hatching is a series of parallel lines. Drawing the lines closer together creates darker tones.

Crosshatching is when a second set of parallel lines crisscrosses the first. Closer lines create darker tones.

Practice

Practice these techniques by shading some objects, such as a cube or a cylinder.

First choose the direction of the light (light source).

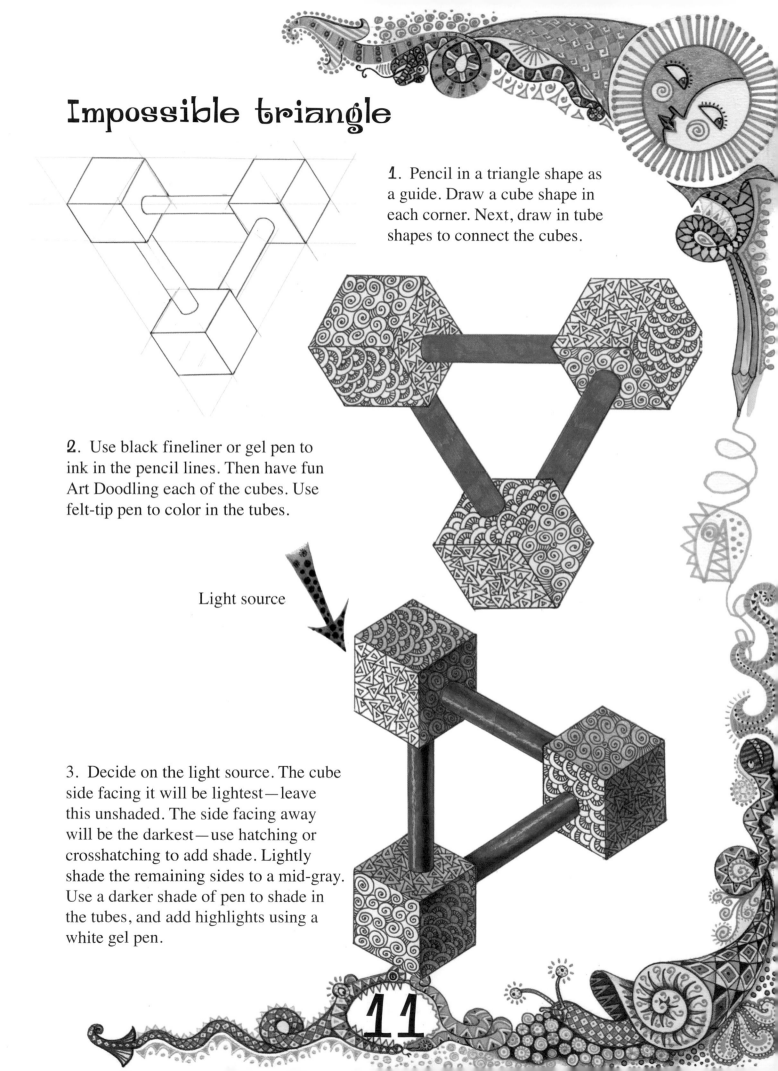

Impossible triangle

1. Pencil in a triangle shape as a guide. Draw a cube shape in each corner. Next, draw in tube shapes to connect the cubes.

2. Use black fineliner or gel pen to ink in the pencil lines. Then have fun Art Doodling each of the cubes. Use felt-tip pen to color in the tubes.

Light source

3. Decide on the light source. The cube side facing it will be lightest—leave this unshaded. The side facing away will be the darkest—use hatching or crosshatching to add shade. Lightly shade the remaining sides to a mid-gray. Use a darker shade of pen to shade in the tubes, and add highlights using a white gel pen.

3D hand

This amazing optical illusion uses a pattern of curving lines to create the impression of a 3D hand. To add impact to this deception, the pattern lines are drawn so they appear to curl up like a sheet of paper unrolling.

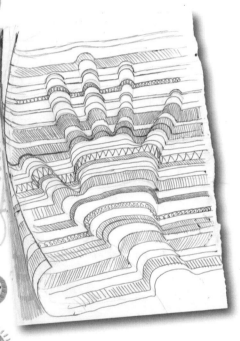

Make a rough sketch on scrap paper. Practice drawing a 3D hand design following steps 1–2.

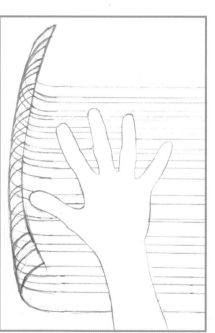

1. Place your hand flat on a sheet of paper. Trace around it in pencil. Now draw a series of horizontal lines as shown. Draw in the curled edge and add curved lines as above.

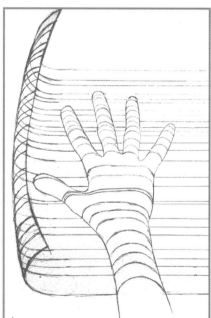

2. Bridge the gap between the horizontal lines, using curving lines that appear to wrap around the hand shape.

3. Use black fineliner or gel pen to go over the pencil lines. Erase pencil marks.

4. Now have fun Art Doodling! Leave a white strip between each pattern line.

Add shading!

13

What do you see?

In this visual illusion you will either see two faces or a vase. If your eyes focus on the black part of the picture you will see an image created by the black shapes, and if you focus on the white part you will see another created by the white shapes. However hard you try, you will be unable to see a vase and two faces both at the same time!

Draw the profile of a face, then trace it in reverse. Place the drawings far apart. As you move them closer, the space in between them takes the shape of a vase.

1. Trace the two drawings onto black paper. Cut them out. Place them on a sheet of white paper as shown. Stick in position.

Do white profiles on black paper to see if you get the same effect!

2. Use a fine, white gel pen to Art Doodle delicate patterns over the black profiles. For the illusion to work, it is important that the contrast between black and white areas is maintained.

3. Now use a pale gray fineliner or fine silver gel pen to Art Doodle patterns over the white areas.

Endless loops

This dynamic design works incredibly well in black and white, as shown in this rough sketch. However, the use of vivid, contrasting colors such as red and green adds subtlety to the design and provides a vibrant base for Art Doodling exciting patterns.

Rough sketch

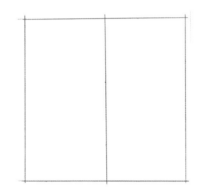

1. Pencil in a square. Add a vertical line through the center.

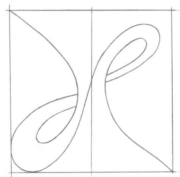

2. Draw in two curving loops as shown.

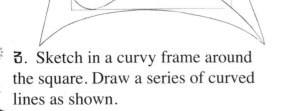

3. Sketch in a curvy frame around the square. Draw a series of curved lines as shown.

4. Carefully add more curved lines to each section of the design until completed as shown.

5. Now go over the finished design in black fineliner or gel pen. Erase any pencil lines. Use watercolor paint or felt-tip pens to color in alternate stripes in green or red. Start Art Doodling using darker shades of green and red fineliner pens.

6. Draw a square frame around the finished design. Art Doodle it with a black and white herringbone pattern. Pencil shading in the corners adds 3D impact!

Geometric 3D

This eye-popping design can be broken down into simple, easy-to-draw steps. Try out different color combinations by making a color rough of your design.

Color rough

1. Pencil in a square. Add diagonal lines.

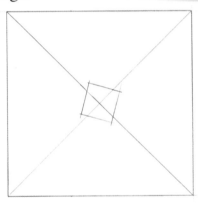

2. Draw a small square in the center, angled slightly as shown.

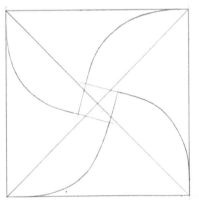

3. Draw curving lines from the small square out to each of the corners.

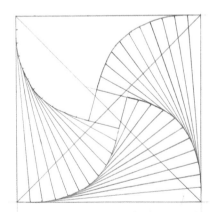

4. Concentrate on one section at a time. Draw a series of radiating lines as shown. Repeat this step until the design is complete.

5. Go over the finished design in black fineliner or gel pen. Erase any pencil marks. Draw a curved, asymmetrical frame around your design. Follow the step-by-step guide (page 22) to Art Doodle the border pattern.

19

Eye trickery

The impression of the snake's body undulating in and out is created by simply alternating the direction of the curved lines. The illusion of the domed eyeball thrusting out of the cube is also based on curved lines.

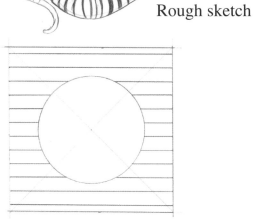

Rough sketch

Drawing the dome

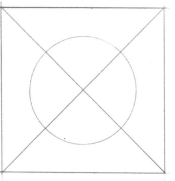

1. Pencil in a square. Draw diagonal lines to find the center. Use compasses to draw a circle.

2. Use a ruler to divide the square into about 12 equal portions. Draw in horizontal lines as shown.

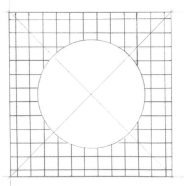

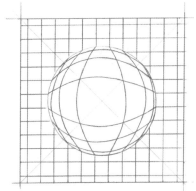

3. Repeat step 2 using vertical lines. Leave the circle blank.

4. Create the illusion of a domed shape by drawing curved lines over the circle as shown.

Draw in the snake (see page 22). Use green and black fineliner and gel pens to Art Doodle the cube. Use yellow, gold, orange, black, and gray for the snake.

Deep color and highlights make a focal point of the reptilian eyes.

Pattern builder

These step-by-step examples show how to Art Doodle some of the patterns used in this book.

Geometric 3D (Pages 18-19)

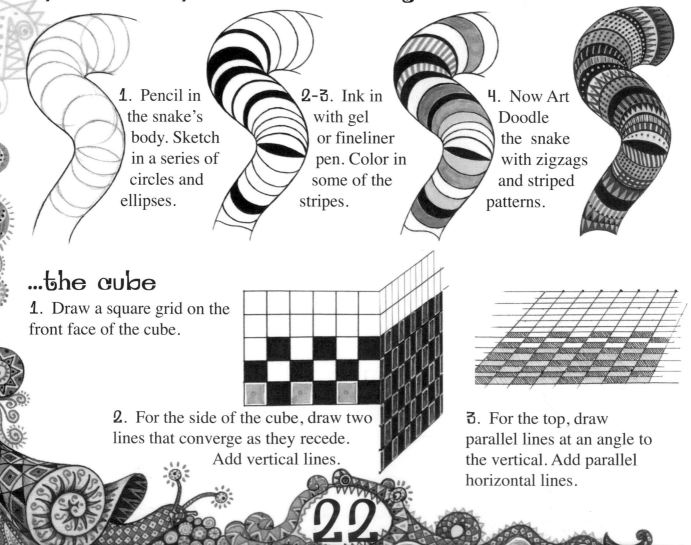

1. Draw 2 horizontal lines, then a triangle shape. Add a third horizontal line.

2. Add a second set of parallel lines to each side of the triangles as shown.

3. Follow the line pattern as shown. Art Doodle in the light, mid, and dark tones.

Eye trickery... the snake (Pages 20-21)

1. Pencil in the snake's body. Sketch in a series of circles and ellipses.

2-3. Ink in with gel or fineliner pen. Color in some of the stripes.

4. Now Art Doodle the snake with zigzags and striped patterns.

...the cube

1. Draw a square grid on the front face of the cube.

2. For the side of the cube, draw two lines that converge as they recede. Add vertical lines.

3. For the top, draw parallel lines at an angle to the vertical. Add parallel horizontal lines.

Glossary

2D two-dimensional; flat.

3D three-dimensional; a 3D drawing gives the illusion of a solid object, even though the drawing itself is flat.

Asymmetrical not matching or balancing on each side of a central axis.

Compasses an instrument for drawing circles and arcs.

Contrasting colors those that differ strongly from one another, such as red and green, blue and orange, yellow and violet.

Crosshatching a crisscrossing of fine parallel lines, used to create dense shading.

Focal point the main center of interest in a work of art.

Hatching a series of fine, parallel lines, used to create light or moderate shading.

Light source the direction from which the light seems to come in a drawing. To give a 3D effect, shading is applied to the surfaces that face away from the light source.

Optical illusion an image that tricks the eye into seeing something different from what is really there— even something that is not possible in real life.

Rough a quick sketch of the main elements in a picture, useful for trying out ideas before starting on the final artwork.

Shading the lines or marks used to fill in areas or represent gradations of colour or tone. Shading is one of the most effective ways to make a drawing look three-dimensional.

Sketch a preparatory drawing; often a quick drawing of a real scene or object that will later be used as inspiration for an original work of art.

Surreal belonging to a 20th-century art movement that portrayed dreamlike images in a realistic way. Well-known Surrealists include Salvador Dalí, René Magritte, and Max Ernst.

Technique an accepted method used to produce a particular result.

Index